THE
RETURNING
SUN:

Hope for a Broken World

George A. Maloney, S.J.

LIVING FLAME PRESS
BOX 74 LOCUST VALLEY, N.Y. 11560

Cover: Robert Manning

Imprimi Potest: Rev. Vincent M. Cooke, S.J.
Provincial of the New York Province
May 2, 1982

Published by: Living Flame Press/Box 74/Locust Valley, New York 11560.

ISBN: 0-914544-42-X

Printed in the United States of America.

Dedication

To the members of
Contemplative Ministries

Acknowledgements

Sincere thanks to Mrs. Rita Ruggiero for typing the manuscript and to Sister Joseph Agnes, S.C.H. for her careful reading and correcting of the manuscript and for other suggestions that proved most helpful.

Excerpts from THE JERUSALEM BIBLE, copyright © 1966 by Darton, Longman & Todd and Doubleday & Company, Inc. Used by permission of the publisher. All scriptural texts are from this Bible version unless otherwise noted.

Some poems were previously published in the following volumes: "Oh, God!" from INSCAPE; "I Surrender" and "Fire Fly" from INVADED BY GOD; "Nearest the Heart of the Father" from JESUS SET ME FREE; "A Valentine Heart," "Broken But Loved," "God Alone," "A Broken Church," "Deep Darkness," "Jesus Tempted," "Desert Poverty," "Healing Love" from BROKEN BUT LOVED.

Author's Foreword

> Rise up in splendor! Your light has come, the glory
> of the Lord shines upon you (Isaiah 60:1).[1]

As the sun sets in all its radiant glory, God shines in the magnificence of its splendor. As the sun again rises and returns to begin a new day, so does Christ return to us daily. Broken though we are in a shattered world, He draws us up to His presence, when we become love to others. It is then that the sun really does return. It is this sun rising that brings hope to our broken world. It is Christ as Light Risen, who leads us to our eternal glory.

Yet most of us go through life totally or partially blind to God's beauty, waiting to be found everywhere, shining "diaphanously" (to use Teilhard de Chardin's term) throughout the entire material world but only to be seen by those who have the eyes to see. Jesus Christ, the Returning Sun, came to heal God's people of their blindness. He came so that man might see.

> But I will make the blind walk along the road and
>   lead them along paths.
> I will turn darkness into light before them and rocky

[1]New American Bible

5

places into level tracks. . . .
Listen, you deaf!
Look and see, you blind! *(Isaiah 42:16-18).*[2]

We Christians have been called by Christ to see Him everywhere as the Light of God's loving presence. We have been called as man, made in His image and likeness, to grasp boldly the Sun in all its brightness, so that we may image His light fully to the world. We become the creative power of God as His word tumbles forth from the lips of the Almighty. That word, spoken in the flowers, the trees, birds, animals, the beauties of each new season, the sun, moon, stars, the mountains, lakes, oceans, goes forth and "shall not return empty" *(Isaiah 55:11).*[3] Truly not only "by the word of the Lord the heavens were made" *(Psalm 33:6),*[4] "but the whole universe has been created in God's Word" *(Colossians 1:16).*[5] Nothing exists or moves toward perfection except by God's creative power immanently present in all things. "In Him we live, and move, and have our being" *(Acts 17:28).*[6]

SITTING IN DARKNESS

We do see things and yet we do not see them. We see beautiful flowers and fail to see the beautiful face of God shining through them. We see men and women, as the blind man of Bethsaida confessed, as "trees . . .

[2]*Ibid*
[3]*Ibid*
[4]*Ibid*
[5]*Ibid*
[6]*Ibid*

6

walking about" *(Mark 8:24).* So much of God's loving presence walks into our lives each day, at each moment, but we fail to see Him, the Returning Sun. We are invaded, bombarded, penetrated constantly by God's energizing love in each event and at each moment. Yet most of us are asleep to that presence. Jesus still shouts out to us: "Why are you asleep? Get up!" *(Luke 22:46).*

When Jesus came among us in the form of a suffering Servant, He announced the Good News about the Kingdom of God. He died for love of us but only in order that He might enter into a new creation when the Father raised Him in His humanity to share divine glory and gave Him the power to pour out God's very own Spirit of Love upon us. In that Spirit we are able to penetrate into the very marrow of all things, to find God at the heart of matter. And, each time we rise to His presence by being love to others, the Sun really does return.

THE SPIRIT OF LIGHT

This Spirit of the risen Jesus "reaches the depths of everything, even the depths of God" *(I Corinthians 2:10).* It is thus that we are taught by God's very own Spirit of Love to find God easily everywhere. This Spirit allows us to touch the very depths of God living the triune life within us. "In the same way the depths of God can only be known by the Spirit of God. Now instead of the spirit of the world, we have received the Spirit that comes from God, to teach us to understand the gifts that he has given us. Therefore we teach . . . in the way that the Spirit teaches us: we teach spiritual things spiritually" *(I Corinthians 2:11-13)*.

It is through the power of Jesus Christ's Spirit that our hidden selves are to grow strong, that Christ is to live in our hearts through faith. We are to go through this beautifully created world that God has given to us and find Him shining through each atom as we are in touch with His Word, the *Logos*. In that *Logos,* and through the Spirit, we are able to grasp the breadth and length, the height and depth of the love of Christ. The Spirit of the risen Saviour will fill us with the "utter fullness of God" *(Ephesians 3:16-19)*.

This is a collection of poem-meditations that I have written in the spirit of the Eastern Fathers. These Fathers were men of prayer, mystics filled with the Spirit of their Lord, Jesus Christ. They could move equally from the study of man and of the events in all creation, to the study of Holy Scripture through various levels of God's revealing presence and loving activity. All too often, we in the West tend to view the unfolding of our lives through the three spatial dimensions of length, breadth and depth and the temporal dimensions of past, present and future. And all too often our relationship to God is similarly expressed and lived in such confining terms.

The Eastern Fathers, because they were mystics, had the ability to view the history of salvation from the unified perspective of God. They could transplant themselves to a higher vantage point and could view the continuity of events from the Old Testament to the New Testament to their own day in the light of the all encompassing present moment, the *now* of God. Though they knew they were situated in the time that unfolded after the historical Person, the *Logos* Incarnate, had already come to earth, they also knew that they were in the present moment as regards God's love.

God's uncreated energies of love surrounded them as they do ourselves. God is in a dynamic process of always revealing Himself to us in the context of our daily, material existence. This eternal, uncreated act of love is always constant, whether in the first moment of creating this universe, or man, or in developing man after the fall, or in the first moment of the physical incarnation of Christ, or in the glorified life of the risen Christ now present, immersed immanently in this universe of ours.

A LOGOS MYSTICISM

Today we are in contact with the religious classics and with spiritual masters of other religions more ancient than Christianity. The same Spirit always has been and still is working in the hearts of all men, who have without exception been made by God according to His image and likeness that is Jesus Christ. This Holy Spirit comes to us and creates and forms us into "deiform," divinized beings, permeated by the divine trinitarian energies working and loving within us.

But it is in and through the *Logos* made flesh, Jesus Christ, that we have the amazing assurance that our assimilation into the Godhead makes it possible that we enter into our true uniqueness, not by absorption, but by the love we experience in the Father through the Son in His Spirit and by the love we then have for each person and creature made by God in and through the *Logos*.

In every mystic tradition the experience of the Absolute becomes more unified, less diffused. The separation is the false ego; the union takes place between the true *I* and its being in the *Other* who is ultimate and has no equal. But the Spirit of Jesus makes it possible for the Christian contemplative to become aware of himself or herself, not as a subject, adoring a divine object, but as the *I*, aware of itself as a child of God, a divinized being participating, as St. Peter says *(II Peter 1:4)* in the divine nature while not losing its human nature, not becoming God by nature, but nonetheless becoming truly deified by God's loving presence within. True Christian contemplatives become aware of this when they experience God deep down as the core of their very being. In the depths of their being He is found as a Person, closer to us than we are to ourselves, as He penetrates us completely.

What contemplative has not experienced in this assimilation that which St. Maximus the Confessor and so many other mystics have described in their analogy of iron and fire?[7] The iron and fire are found together in a fiery sword, but the piece of iron effects exactly that which is in accordance with its own nature. It glows as fire, but in a way that is proper to iron. The glowing sword cuts and burns at the same time; as iron it cuts, as fire it burns.

We Christians are given the fantastic privilege by faith of actually being immersed into the fire of the *Logos* both in profound, contemplative prayer and in the Eucharist which cannot really be separated as two distinct moments

[7]St. Maximus: *Ambigua* 5; p. 91; 1060A

of loving adoration. Yet the *Logos* incarnated does not come to us alone. He is, by His essence as *Logos, relational.* He points to the Father, and He points from the Father to us. "I am in the Father and the Father is in me" *(John 14:10).* Where Christ, the Divine Son, is, there also is the Father. And where the Father and the Son are present, there also is the Holy Spirit, who loves the Father and the Son within us and with us.

I have tried to capture in several of the poems in this collection, the trinitarian presence within us and a sense of the privilege we have of surrendering to such a loving family. "Oh, God!" rises easily from our lips and hearts as we contemplate this indwelling Father, Son and Spirit, pouring out Their relational personhood as our unique Father, Brother and Spirit of love.

JESUS THE LORD

In other poems, I have tried to capture what Jesus Christ means to me and to other Christians as He becomes Lord and Master of our lives. Here again the Fathers of the desert have guided my experience of what the Incarnation should mean, that God should become man in order that man might become God, as Saint Irenaeus of the second century wrote. He who was from all eternity one with God did not deem it an honor to hold on to but He emptied Himself, taking upon Himself the form of a suffering servant, obedient unto death, the death of the cross *(Philippians 2:6-8).*

In Eastern Christian spirituality there has always been a special accent on the gentleness and humility of the Word made flesh as He comes to serve us in order to reflect the infinite love of the Father. He serves us not in power but in the weakness of a suffering servant on the cross. This is the *kenotic* spirituality of the Eastern mystics who (in Saint Paul's words, "He emptied himself," *Philippians 2:7*) strove to live a life of nonviolence and of gentle and humble service in imitation of the suffering servant of Yahweh.

We can learn from the wise men of the Eastern deserts who found, through constant repetition of the name of Jesus, the means to remain consciously in His healing presence. This repetition and recollection of the name of Jesus and His risen presence living within the individual Christian become true prayer of the heart only when the pronouncement of the Name is accompanied by a quickening consciousness of the indwelling Lord. By reverently pronouncing the Name of Jesus, we too can begin to experience His presence in a more vital way.

THE HEALING DIVINE PHYSICIAN

In the presence of the indwelling Lord we are able to enter into the deeper reaches of our psyche and there, in the desert of our hearts, we can encounter the "demonic" forces: the brokenness, the fears and unforgiveness of times past and humbly cry out to the Lord Jesus to come and have mercy on us and heal us. "Lord, Jesus Christ, Son of God, have mercy on me, a sinner!"

Jesus Christ will plunge down deeply into our consciousness, and even our unconscious, into all parts of our mind and heart and take possession of all parts of our being in powerful healing, but only if we cry out incessantly that He come and be Lord of our consciousness and unconscious. We will stand attentive and vigilant over every thought as we strive to bring everything within our "hearts" into the healing power of His love. "Every thought is our prisoner, captured to be brought into obedience to Christ. Once you have given your complete obedience, we are prepared to punish any disobedience" *(II Corinthians 10:5-6)*.

By entering into the "womb-tomb" of our hearts, we can open ourselves in faith to Jesus who still heals according to our belief *(Mark 11:24)*. Jesus Christ can still be encountered as the healing, Divine Physician, for He lives deep within our "hearts" and He promised that He and the Father would come and abide within us *(John 14:23)*. At the center of our being we can still fall down and confess our belief that Jesus Christ is the Son of God. We can cry out to Him that we are broken in body, soul and spirit. It is at this point that we will truly believe and actually experience a healing transformation.

In deep prayer we learn to surrender to His love and peace, letting it pour over us like a soft rain falling gently on dry ground. Our potential for *being* expands into a realized consciousness. We feel in the depths of our being a transformation taking place. Power to love, to *be* toward God, ourselves and others, in a healthy way, opens up slowly like a lotus flower. Jesus can set us free of the chaotic past and empower us by His Spirit to go forth to be a healing force to all the persons we are privileged to meet and serve.

God humbly ties His healing power of love to the love of Him experienced in us in prayer that urges us to incarnate the same Word enfleshed Love of Jesus Christ in the lives of others. The Eastern Fathers have always stressed in line with the vision of Saint Paul especially, that if we are in Christ we participate in His paschal victory over sin and death. We are a new creation in Him and are empowered to become with Him and His Spirit a reconciler of the whole world.

> And for anyone who is in Christ, there is a new creation; the old creation has gone, and now the new one is here. It is all God's work. It was God who reconciled us to himself through Christ and gave us the work of handing on this reconciliation. . . . So we are ambassadors for Christ; it is as though God were appealing through us, and the appeal that we make in Christ's name is: be reconciled to God *(II Corinthians 5:17-20).*

THE LIGHT OF CHRIST

To the degree that the process of transformation takes place in us, so also will the liberating, illuminating, kindling spark of the Infinite Light shine more and more frequently until finally it becomes an integral part of our daily life. One of the basic themes found in the New Testament, especially in the Johannine writings, is that Christ is Light and we Christians, when we have surrendered to his indwelling presence and Lordship, become Light also as we share in the transforming power of Christ. The Eastern Fathers, climaxed by Saint Gregory Palamas, stress how Christians, even in this life, can participate in the Taboric Light that shone on Christ in His transfiguration on Mount Tabor.

We Christians can experience the fullness of our

Baptism as we move literally out of our existential darkness of self-centeredness into the light of God's Allness. This illumination of the heart flows from an act of the Holy Spirit who is God's divinizing Light. The indwelling Spirit brings us into an awareness that we are really children of God. He effects the likeness of Jesus Christ within us. He is the one who draws out the potentiality locked within us, as in a seed, to become transfigured into the very Body of the Risen Lord, Jesus.

Through the effects of this inner illumination, our whole being becomes radiant. Under the radiation of the divine energies, experienced through the illumination of the Holy Spirit, the energies of the "heart" are vivified in their turn and the inner transfiguration transfigures us into children of God. I have tried to recapture, in some of the following poems, the theme of a sharing even now in this life which is repeated so often in the writings of the Eastern Fathers. Resurrection is already ours; we have entered into a sharing already, an anticipation, of the future resurrection as we die daily to our own selfishness and rise to let the power of Jesus' resurrection dominate and direct our lives in greater self-sacrificing love toward our neighbors.

I ask the reader's pardon if he or she does not find the following poem-meditations "high" poetry. I humbly offer them as sparks that might enkindle a flame of great fire within the heart of the reader. I am bold to offer them because I feel that they reflect some of the insights of the Eastern Fathers, which lie more in the area of insightful prayer rather than in clear and distinct ideas. "Doing theology" for them, and hopefully for us, involves listening to the Spirit and allowing Him to reveal to us the Father and Son, in an experience that divinizes us more and more into loving children of so loving a Heavenly Father.

The great prophet who wrote Chapter 60 of the Book of Isaiah comes closest to the vision behind the following poem-meditations. I pray they will dispose the reader to move in deep prayer from darkness toward the transcendent light of God's presence that is shining from within you and outside you throughout all of creation.

Arise, shine out, for your light has come,
the glory of Yahweh is rising on you,
though night still covers the earth
and darkness the peoples.

Above you Yahweh now rises
and above you his glory appears.
The nations come to your light
and kings to your dawning brightness.

. . . .

At this sight you will grow radiant,
your heart throbbing and full;
since the riches of the sea will flow to you,
the wealth of the nations come to you;

. . . .

No more will the sun give you daylight,
nor moonlight shine on you,
but Yahweh will be your everlasting light,
your God will be your splendour.

Your sun will set no more
nor your moon wane,
but Yahweh will be your everlasting light
and your days of mourning will be ended.

Your people will all be upright,
possessing the land for ever;
a shoot that Yahweh has planted,
my handiwork, designed for beauty.

Isaiah 60:1-3; 5-6; 19-21.

George A. Maloney, S.J.
February 3, 1982

Contents

Oh, God!

I sit in early morn
and gaze on my God.
I see the light of His smile
in the soft rays of the dawn
that tiptoe into my room.
His light covers me
and warms me.
I stir to His presence
    around me,
      within me.

The cocoon that so many years
of silent births and deaths has
spun into a prison
begins to split down its sides.
Slowly, His loving energies
pour over me.
I stretch toward life.
I move toward light
from out my hibernating darkness.

Oh, God! You gave me wings!
They unfold, wet and packed-tight,
to spangled colors of rainbow fair.
God, was all this beauty and power
always there, locked inside?
Were You always present,
warm Light of piercing love?
Why so long to be called to life?
Why so much prison cell confining?
Where were You, God?

Son, know that My love is eternal.
My presence can never become absence.
My Light can never turn to darkness.
My Spring is never Winter.
I have always encompassed you
with My energies of love.
I live within you.
I am the Force around you.
You can never be outside
of My Uncreated Love.

But it is you
who in womb-tomb
had to open up to My Life.
You had to want
    Light over darkness,
    Life over death,
    Love over fear.

In due time, I sent
    My spring-warmth into your life.
I laughed through their eyes.
I encircled you in their arms.
I breathed My Life in their breath
and you came forth in love.
Oh, God!
Let Your energies bathe me today.
May Your light encompass me.
Fill me with Your loving presence.
Send me Your love again,
that I may stretch
my colored wings
    out and up
    and fly in ecstasy
    dizzily up into the heavens,

leaving the bonds of this earth behind,
in remembrance of what was.

Oh, God!
Be Spring again!
Let Winter finish,
ne'er to return.
Let only Your Love
reign supreme.
Bring me, again, Your Life!

God-Woman

As I jogged in early morn,
I looked up and saw You, God!
You were woman, total woman,
as You stretched out on the couch
    of the heavens above at early dawn.
Your long white hair tumbled
over Your hidden face
like shook foil, dappled brilliantly
by shafts from rising sun.
I listened in awe
as You groaned in painful love
to bring to birth
    the gift of this new day!

Thanksgiving

Thank You, loving Father,
for the sunrise lived today.
The sky was spangled
with broken clouds,
pink-hued
promise of more to come.

Then suddenly the flaming ball
danced and quivered
and in a burst
there it was, all fire!

Human love is like that.
Clouds hiding all that.
And then there it is —
All fire!

I wait eagerly
for the sunset tonight.
If there can be
so much delicateness
in the sunrise
and so much heat at noon,
My God, what will
Your sunset be!

I Surrender

I pray alone
on the mountaintops of night.
It is so calm, so still.
All is dark;
yet coming closer and closer
to me is a robe
of great brilliance.
I close my eyes in fear.
As the full Sun,
He stops before me,
dazzling, dancing.
His presence pierces
through my whole being
like fire searing, burning
yet consuming me not.
I kiss the earth before Brilliance.
I let go and fly to ecstasy.
Oh, God, before such beauty
I surrender!

Fire Fly

Fire fly, dancing in the dark,
what makes you glow so?
O *Phosphoros*, Light-bearer,
is it because the light of Christ
    shines in you, through you
    to lighten up the darkness?

Why is there light,
    and then the silent darkness
    soon broken by soft light?
Why not total light
    all the time
    dispelling all the night's darkness?

O Christ, be the light,
Phos Hilaron, Radiant Light,
    that I may carry
    into the world's darkness.
Make me a carrier of Your light,
    that I too may be
    flashing light across the night.

In the night I stretch out
    to embrace Your light.
Come, Bright Light of Love,
    phosphorize my being!
May Your light be total,
    not on or off,
    but may it consume
    the darkness in me.

Fire fly, flash away in the night.
For full day soon will be here.
And no one will see your light
    until there returns again the night.

O Christ, be full noon to me,
or if night must be,
may Your light be constant,
    not flashing, off and on.
May I carry Your light,
    be Your light to others
    who sleep in the dark of night.

God's Gift of the Spirit

In early morn
God lifted me to a mountaintop.
He splashed the east
with hues of violet,
pink and bleeding red.

I cried:
"Stop, Lord, such beauty
brings my heart to breaking point!"
I bathed in His warm light.
His love drove the chill
from out of my heart.
I was one with Him,
the Source of life.

Then He made me
to lie down, as to sleep.
Like an operating surgeon,
with deft fingers, strong and tender,
He drew out of me a form.
In the twilight I could not see.
He placed it next to me
and breathed into it
His life-giving Spirit of Love.
"This is My gift to you.
to cherish and to love.
She will be more beautiful
to you than the flaming sunrise.
No sunset will ever excite you
as the beauty of her lips
or the dancing laughter in her eyes."

I humbled myself before her
and whispered my *yes*.

O God, what You have joined
together in happy union
may no man cut asunder.
May no trial or tribulation
take away the oneness
You have made
when You gave Your Spirit
as Your gift to me.

O, beautiful Gift from God!
I sink myself into the depths
of that infinite love.
I touch, dizzily, heights
that laughingly escape my grasp.
I plunge into depths.
I am You.
You are I.
    We are God's,
one with Him!

30

Nearest the Heart of the Father

The Son is nearest
the heart of the Father.

"In sinu Patris."
He "insinuates" Himself,
enters into the Heart
of His Father.
They embrace,
surround each other,
like a mother covering her baby,
like two lovers made one
in ecstatic embrace.

O God, cover me!
Embrace me!
Make me one,
as You and Jesus are one.
Draw me into Your Heart.
Immerse me deeply into Yourself.

If human love can heal
all division and separation,
if lovers know only oneness,
what must it be
to be nearest
the Heart of the Father,
"In sinu Patris?"

Pentecost

No one has ever seen the wind.
It is in blown trees
and tossled hair,
skirts lifted high
and feverish brows cooled
that we see in the sign
the presence of the wind.

No one has ever seen God's Spirit.
It is in His words
spoken in silence,
in human hands touched with tenderness;
it is in the oneness
of two lovers
surrendering to each other
that the Spirit is known as Love.

O Spirit of Love,
come upon me today.
Melt me
into a new oneness.
Be a wind that blows
far from me
all selfishness and division.
Leave only the clean-swept
plains of my soul,
freed at last of all debris.

It is only in Your aliveness
to make us alive

to each other
that we know
Your Otherness
and know too
that two make one
in Your melting presence.

Lead us down
into the dark cavern
of our hearts.
There in the watery womb
like foetus and mother,
may we know
neither separateness
nor division.

Come, O Spirit,
and baptize us.
Let Your living waters
stir us to new life.
Let Your fire enfold
us and enflame us
with a baptism of love.
May we live for each other
and thus know the love of God
as Spirit that makes
all love possible,
as love that knows
only union, deep
communion,
eternal oneness in being.

Finding God in You

I searched day and night
to look upon Your face, O God.
Was it there in the early morning dew
that diamonded in shattered light
rays so soft in hue?

Or did I see You in the even sunset
as You splashed the west
with colors rainbow-tossed?
I looked into the face of baby,
youth, man and woman
and saw pain and fear, but God,
when would You appear?

Then one day Your gift came into my life
like velvet step of early dawn.
Before such beauty I trembled.
Could it be true, O God,
that You would bend so close to me
and in loving touch
tell me that You are love?

In gentle, warm embrace
Your arms that hold the heavens above
surround me in sacred whisper
that You too love me.

With breathless waiting
like eagle poised, ready for flight
into the storm-raging skies

I look again for Your face, O God,
for Your tender embrace
and soft, loving kiss,
as darkened clouds dispel
and sunkist sky bursts forth
in smile again
and in the gift of the other.

Beyond Time

There is no time
for what we share.
For it at once
encompasses all time
and
I, a guest,
in my own time,
wait,
knowing You
beyond time.

A Valentine Heart

St. Valentine's Day,
a day for lovers
to remember
that love means death,
that love means a giving
of self to another
who becomes more important to you
than your own self.

This is a day to recall
the heart of You, O my God.
No one has ever loved
as You love me.
No one has ever suffered
so much in pained heart
as You who have given me
all in the love of Jesus emptied.

O Jesus!
Yours is the heart
closest to the heart of the Father.
Your pierced and emptied heart
mirrors for me the self-emptying
of the Father's love for me.
He knows in You
that love is pain.
It is suffering.
It is death.
It is self-forgetting.
It is living for the other.

It is truly a pierced heart,
emptied of all from within.

O, Father and Son,
pour into my heart
Your humble Spirit
of gentleness and patience,
of love, peace and joy,
that I, too, may learn
to love with Your love
the other selves, my true selves
that You have gifted me
to love as I love myself.

May my heart offered to them
become a pierced heart,
a suffering heart,
as I slowly learn
that love is death
but it is also true life!

Paradox of Love

Into our broken world
You came, Lord Jesus.
You embraced our darkness,
even though You are pure light.
You were born in a cave
and wrapt in flimsy cloth,
You who cover the heavens
with the sun, moon and stars.
You cried for Your mother's milk,
You who fed the entire world.
You needed the warm arms of a mother,
You who stretch out to embrace the universe.
You submitted to the Law,
You who make all laws of nature.
You were baptized as a sinner in the Jordan,
You who are sinless and all pure.
You traveled about preaching to the multitudes,
You who are the silent, everlasting Word of God.
You touched the lepers,
gave sight to the blind,
opened the ears of the deaf,
because You came to give them abundant life.

You, the King of the universe,
became like a humble servant.
You were hungry and thirsty,
You who provide food and drink for all.
Sinners touched You
and were healed of their loneliness.
You were called a friend of harlots,

You the pure Bridegroom of Your Church.
You were poor with no pillow for Your head,
You who possess the fullness of the Father.

You were the Light,
but the darkness did not comprehend.
You offered love,
but received rejection in turn.
You wept for the sins of the world,
You, the Joy of the world.
You washed the feet of sinful men,
the Master who came to serve.
Ours were the sufferings You bore,
ours the sorrows You carried.
You were struck low
as a criminal, crushed for our sins.
You were acquainted with sorrows,
You who brought pleasure to Your Father.
Your sufferings and punishment
bring to us peace and forgiveness.
And by Your wounds
    we can be healed.

O, Jesus, radiant Light,
You entered into our darkness
of sin, violence and shame,
that we might have a share
in Your healing light.
On the cross, like a valiant warrior,
You entered into the battle
of Light against darkness,
of love against selfishness,
of giving against possessing.

The soldiers looked upon You
   whom they had pierced,
for they saw that to break Your bones
was useless, for You were total brokenness.
You were taken down from the cross,
wrapt again in flimsy cloth
and held in the arms of Your Mother.

"Jerusalem, Jerusalem,
what more could I do for you?"

God has reached the limit
of giving, of self-emptying.
No shade of blackness could be
added to Your darkness.
No more void to absolute Zero!

O God, in Jesus may I learn
that love becomes fiery light
only in the total, broken darkness.

Healing Love

I walked along the quiet mountain road.
The full moon laughed with joy
while the rest of nature slept.
I entered into a crevice
of a rock near the stream.

There was peace.
But then I felt God's presence
slowly come upon me.
Faster and faster He pursued me.
I wasn't running from Him.

I was entering into Him!

Deeper and deeper
I plunged!
I knew that somehow
when I left this place
I would always remain
in that crevice,
so full of God's peace and joy.

I had touched God.
I had found Heaven on earth!
God's Spirit had come upon me
in that moonlit evening
as I hid in the arms
of God, my Beloved!

Oh, what healing Love
comes over my brokenness!

All healing comes from God
in the desert cave
when I, in brokenness,
call out to You, Divine Physician.

I will never be the same
since You touched me
and I hid in Your healing arms.
New powers awake
as spring-clarion sounds
within the depths of that crevice,
the rock of my heart.

Locked-in petals
of a bedewed rose
gently let go
to unveil a new harmony
of many things captured
in the union of one flower
of exquisite beauty.

The chaotic past, dried bones
of long yester-years,
receive the soft breath
of God's Spirit of Love.

And they become enfleshed
into a living being.
I come out of the past
as I cry to my Lord;
"Lord, Jesus Christ, Son of God,
have mercy on me
a sinner!"

Like butterfly bursting
forth in melted gold
with wet, tightly-packed wings,
I stretch upward.
Dry wings strengthen
and lift me aloft
to new, dizzying heights
of union with God.

But then I hear
that healing voice
say to me,
"Go to your broken
brothers and sisters.
Stretch out your hands
on their pain-ridden bodies.

"Give My healing Love
to all that you meet.
Be My hands and feet
that can, like Shepherd,
gather again the scattered sheep
and bring them to My Father."

Broken but healed
I step out in faith
to be a broken healer
to a broken world.

Desert Poverty

Heavenly Father!
May Your loving Spirit
drive me deeper and deeper
into the arid, sterile desert
of my inmost being.
And there in prayer and fasting
may I become hungry
to feed upon Your life-giving Word.

God, how often I, too, am tempted
to turn stones into bread,
to take Your freely bestowed gifts
and use them to feed
my false security, to hide behind
my true nothingness,
before the Allness of Your loving presence.

Father, in my great need
to assert my identity
before myself, the world and even You,
may I never yield to the temptation
to take Your powers given to me
and use them for my own selfish ends.

But may I be rich in my poverty,
enlightened in my darkness,
fed in my hunger
be Your living Word, Jesus.

May You teach me and the Church
how to be poor, to serve the poor,
to overcome every temptation to be falsely rich
by misusing Your gifts,
given only to lovingly serve Your poor.

In my inner poverty and emptiness
that only the desert can reveal to me,
may I learn that true food
is not power, but only Your Word,
to obey by loving service to others poor.

May Your gift of the Bread of Life,
that You send down upon Your *Anawim,*
like manna newly fallen from Heaven,
be my strength and that of Your Church
to live by Your Word
in loving service to all the poor.

Conversion

The chase is over.
   You found me
    as I hid,
  thinking I was safe.

I fled You,
   burying myself by day in the
lizard holes of the desert,
and by night creeping forth to bathe
   in the pauches of the ocean,
weaving seaweed through my hair,
encrusting myself
   with the jeweled jelly fish
to hide my being.

Then I felt Your breath.
   I clambered the rocks,
haunted the subterranean caves
   letting myself through, piece by piece,
the hidden exits
   to scale the mountains
and be one with the wind,
   to make of myself a breeze
stirring the needles
and arranging the snowflakes
   as they fell on my form.

Wanton and derisive when I heard Your step,
  I fled again to this flat plain.
Here You would not come,

for in the desolation of my desert
and in the elation of my mountain,
    in the soothing of my ocean
You did not prevail.
        I had left You far behind.

But You ARE here!
You have picked me up, a kitten clawing
    and You have gently stroked me into obedience.
You have fed me;
    I have been drunk on Your love.
You have stilled my beating heart;
    my feet are sodden and useless,
    subservient to my knees.
I screamed at You to leave me;
    instead praises spewed forth from my lips.
You made me Your captive;
I flee no more.

Never shall I be as I was before.
Without You — there is no purpose
    to living.
You've left me with a hunger
        only You can satisfy,
        with a restlessness
        only You can soothe,
with a pain
        only You can mitigate,
        with a life
        only You can give,
        with a hope
        only You can fulfill.
I possess You,
yet I must search for You again.

I trace the steps of a wanderer
to the desert
    where I find You not
under the dry bones
    of what I had been.

In the ocean
    there is no soothing.
Naked and without covering
    the seaweed burns
    and the starfish cut.
There is no respite
    from my hurt.
With maddening pace I clamber the rocks
    to search the subterranean caves.
The bats of forgotten denials beat my face,
    the rocks shred afresh my spirit.
I find You not.

My spirit longs for You with an intensity
    beyond description;
with a feeling that is more human
    than life itself.

The pain of wanting You
    will waste my frame and drain my senses.
I shall die,
        but my spirit still will search.

Upon the mountaintop of spirit
    I kneel alone.
There is no further place to go,
    no other place that's yet unsearched.
I wallow in the blackness

for strength is gone,
I can live no more.

The evil in my heart
    makes one tremendous clutch
around my throat
and from the portals of my lips
    one last cry flings skyward.

Above my gasping breath and choking sob,
a touch like falling snowflake
    upon my cheek
relaxes my heaving body.
From within a VOICE, soft as sound of leaf
    floating groundward;
yet strong enough
        to quell my sobbing cries,
murmuring,
    "Welcome home!"

Jesus Tempted

Jesus:
I stand before You,
who are haggard and lean,
from lack of food and drink,
from trials and temptations in the desert.

I see You in the moonlight
as You prostrate Yourself in the olive garden,
torn by fear of death,
of suffering so much
for such little avail.

I approach in the darkness
of Your noon "hour"
and stand beside Your Mother
at the foot of the cross.

You are like a potsherd,
broken, and all spilt out.
"Without beauty, without majesty,"
You are a man of sorrows
familiar with human sufferings.

You truly were tempted,
as we, in all things,
yet You did not sin.

You, the Light of the world,
consented to enter into darkness.
In the struggle to overcome the darkness

around You and within You,
Your holiness became incandescent.
It reached its peak of glory
in the ignominy of Calvary,
when all darkness of self-centeredness
dissolved in the light of Your Father's Love.
"My God, my God!"
in darkest abandonment
brought Your victory cry:
"Father, into Thy hands I commend my spirit."

Lord, Jesus, meek and humble of heart,
meet me in my darkest moments
and, as warm sun gently
scatters darkness and fog,
so come and be my Light.

52

In times of trial and temptation,
be my strength and consolation.
Teach me not to fear the darkness,
but rather draw me to Your Light.

For it can only be in such darkness
that You will become my Light.
And in Your Light,
may I bring the Light
of healing love to all I meet.

Silence

Star differs from star.
And so do silences.
There is the silence
of a forest, no leaf stirring.
There is the silence
before battle as enemies
hold their fire before the kill.
Two lovers reach a union
of love that silences all words.
And then, there is the silence of death.

God's language is silence
as He brings forth a universe
silently over millions of years.
How quietly He is present
in the flight of the butterfly
and in the growth of the stately oak.

But His greatest silence
came into our noisy world
when His Word leapt forth
from God's bursting heart
of love so great
that other words were noise.

That Word spoke of Love in action
as He silently washed the feet
of His disciples and bade
them do the same to others.
He touched the maimed,

the paralytics and the blind
and quietly He healed them
with His love.

But after preaching and teaching
to ears that did not hear,
this Word spoke His last word in silence.

On Calvary the Divine Seed was lifted aloft
and plunged into the earthy hole.
Silently in slow, dying pain
His side split forth.
The Seed seemed to have perished.
The Word was finally silenced.
Yet in that darkened silence
God spoke ever so gently
to those who have ears to hear:

"Here is My love incarnate.
Silence your heart to hear
My Word speak in emptiness
of love poured out, of love divine
that will bring you the power
to speak and hear the Word of love
to all that you meet."

Deep Darkness

Father, frightened, Your child couches
in the depths of darkness and despair.
Fears and tremors, worries and cares
attack him endlessly and he alone
strikes now here, now there,
only to be pummelled by invisible forces
into hopeless prison-like confinement.

From whence come these enemies
to take me into everlasting servitude?
O bitter day that I believed
his name Lucifer meant light-bearer
instead of bearer of darkness and death!

Father, Your child is crying in the night
because he thinks that he is all alone
in darkness and in fear. He does not know
that You are watching still. Send him Your voice
to speak in stillness deep as summer fields
kept windless in the blazing sun of noon
and silvered in the silence of the night,
but yet as loud as thunder. Tell him that
he need but turn to You and You will come
so swiftly he will instantly forget
the years or minutes his identity
in You was unremembered. Who could then
recall the tiny ticks of time in which
the past went by; the fearful thoughts in which
the future was kept carefully concealed
in black unknowingness? Eternity

has come to lift them both away and shine
in quiet certainty in place of time,
and all the little things that time must bring.
Look now upon the child who has forgotten
the meaning of Your Love.

O holy Father of the universe,
Creator of all things that live in You,
in whom not one could ever be forgotten
nor lost in time. The dreaming of the world
will pass away with Your remembrance,
no child of Yours but must remember You.
Yet time must obscure eternity, as truth
seems to be hidden when illusions rise
and veil the face of Christ. It does not seem
to have reality, and You who are
more near than breathing, yet appear to be
remote; unreal, so far the distant stars
seem closer. In long darkness it is hard
to keep faith in the Returning Sun.
Your child is tired. Let him hear Your voice,
and let the rest that sleep can never give be his.

Your child is sad. Remind him of Your Word,
and all the joy that suddenly becomes
Your gift to him is shared by all the world.
He is afraid. But let him hear the sound
of Heaven's reassurance, and the years
of almost hopeless waiting and despair
shrink to a holy instant and be gone.

A Broken Church

God called His people
to be His chosen friends.
If Yahweh set His heart
on you and chose you,
it was not because you
outnumbered other peoples.
You were the least of all peoples.
It was for love of you
that I brought you out of Egypt
and freed you from slavery.

And this alone I asked of you,
that you would keep My commandments
and love one another
as I have loved you.
I promised that you would increase.
I would bless your offspring
and the work of your hands.

But My people have forgotten Me.
They have exchanged My glory
for the darkness of their own idols.
They have abandoned Me, Yahweh,
the Fountain of living water,
only to dig cisterns for themselves
that hold no water.

I sent in due time
My Son to dwell among them.
He came as a light

but the darkness in their hearts
rose up in mock righteousness
and snuffed out the Light of the world.
Yet I glorified Him
and raised Him to new power.
He poured out His Spirit
to breathe My breath of life
into the dry bones of the remnant
of My broken people.

And they rose with Him
to form a part of His Body.
They were the "called-out" assembly,
belonging to Him as the branches
belong to the vine,
He gave them power
to heal the sick and broken,
to give Himself as the Bread of life
to the starving of the world.

They preached the Good News
that He and I are one
and in our Spirit of love
We wanted to make our abode
within them as in a new temple.
They baptized in our triune family,
Father, Son and Spirit.
They brought the saving Word
to nations unto the ends of the world.

I betrothed that people to My Son
as a bride to the Bridegroom.
That bride was virginal and comely,
thrilling the heart of her Spouse.
And yet how she grew restless,

desirous of new riches and power.
She traded His glory
for the tinsel of this world.
She harloted herself
to the princes of this world.

Broken and betrayed, she weeps
in the desert to return to her Spouse.
I will rise and go back
to my first and true Husband.
I will confess my sins.
I will weep for forgiveness
and He will answer my cry.

My Son will take her back.
He will lure her to Himself
and heal her of her brokenness.
He will bring her into new health
with tenderness and love.
And out of her will come
a new progeny of children
more numerous than the stars above
and the grains of sand on the seashore.

This is what My Son will do
if you, My People,
will claim Me as your God
and My Son as your Spouse.

God Alone

Lord, Jesus, I too am alone
in the arid desert of my heart.
It is calm, so still.
Yet all is dark.
Suddenly there flashes
from out the tomb of my heart
a light that dances
laughingly, enticingly.
It coaxes and beckons me
to the brink of the precipice.
"Go ahead and jump!"
a voice shouts deep within.
"You are great and can do no wrong.
God is on your side.
What you think is the very way
that God thinks and approves.
Whatever you want
God will give you
    just as you want it."

Another light brilliantly shining
pierces my inner darkness.
This voice is soft and alluring.
Siren-like it casts over the screen
    of my mind's eye
pictures of places far off,
castles and palaces,
songs and dances, food and drink,
clothes and leisure,
honors and glory,

power and might.
"All this is yours if you will
only promise Me
a little favor, ever so small.
Serve Me as your master.
Want no other
and to you I give
all riches, pleasures and happiness."

O God, like Jesus, may I cry out,
"Away, you tempter!
I belong to God
and Him alone I serve.
To follow your glitter and sham
is to be sucked into the mud
of endless servitude.
Shame and guilt will be my food
as I waste away in prison cell confining."

Only You, O Lord, shall I obey.
In poverty and lowly truth
I shall be lifted up by You
and declared Your loving son
who always pleases You.

Broken But Loved

I join the crowd of broken people,
hobbling, falling, screaming and crying
in their sickness and inner misery.
Frantically we search, now here, now there.
Can no one heal us, bring us new life?
We hang on each other and we pull each other down
into a sharing of misery added to each other's.

What darkness covers my soul!
What bonds hold me imprisoned!
What leprous wounds cover me
and eat my substance away!

O Jesus, Divine Physician, come
and stretch Your healing hands upon me.
Break loose my bonds and set me free.
Dispel the darkness by the Light of Your presence.
Thaw the freezing in all my limbs.
Warm my cold isolation with Your love.

O most gentle, merciful Savior,
bend over me again and enspirit
these dry bones of mine
with Your Spirit that alone brings new life.
Let me feel once more Your healing touch,
that resurrects me from the dead,
that quiets the storm within my breast.
Let Your love sear through me
like an arrow plunged deep down
into the last resistance in my heart.

Lord and Master, how great is Your love,
how ever abiding and everlasting
and, yet, how blinded I was to Your great Light,
how absent to Your surrendering presence.

I cry out, Savior, that You offer again
that healing love that destroys all sin,
that breaks down prison walls of pride
and sends me forth in humble service
to share Your healing love with others.

"Here is My love offered to you,
a love of pain, of suffering unto death.
Take and receive My gift of Self,
My healing stillness that drives
from out your heart all noise and clamor,
My whispering love that shouts to you
of love divine, pursuing, ever present.

"This healing love I give to you.
Kneel down to receive this anointing
as kings of old, as consecrated priests.
I send you forth, healed and whole
to be a healing touch of love
to all you meet.
You were broken, but always loved.

"Now be love to those who still know
not of My healing, loving power.
Tell them the Good News
that darkness can be turned into Light,
that loneliness can embrace and be united
into a loving community of many
in the oneness of My love."
Absence is driven out by presence,
brokenness can be healed by Love!